I Choose to
SSSOAR
BY DENELL PORCHÉ

A Poetry Guide to Somehow, Someway,
with Some Effort Overcoming All Rifts

– Mini - steps create
monumental gain."
~ Smooches, D. P.

Published by Melanie Womack Connections, LLC.

All Melanie Womack Connections, LLC titles, imprints and distributed lines are available at special quantity discounts for bulk purchase for sales promotion premiums, fund-raising, educational, or institutional use.

ISBN 13: 978-0-692-79094-6

First Printing April 2016 Printed in the United States

10 9 8 7 6 5 4 3 2 1

Table of Contents

Preface

This is simply an introductory course to your awakening. I present things to encourage, to inspire. So you may go on your way in a healthy state of mind, discovering yourself on the journey destined for you; for it is you creating the experience along the way. If you are not as healthy in mind as you may think, how are you providing opportunities and tools to support the present being you are.

I am the call to action for a better you. SSSOAR provides pathways to assist in identifying, becoming and/or restructuring a healthier you. Two key concepts, "know, most precious on this earth, you" and "heal, so your world may follow."

Sometimes we need a little encouragement, a reminder to who we are and to whom we belong to. Many times we forget how powerful, how beautiful, how important we are. We all have a place and space in this world. It is knowing and understanding the place we occupy and exist in has come due to our own involvement and in addition, with some occasions, things presented where we have no control over except in how we respond. It is in the mist of these things to remember our capabilities, adjust our thinking, preserver at best, finding our peace in life in every situation. Life happens with us and in most times we have completely forgotten the power of choice and knowing we are safe.

The acronym S.S.S.O.A.R stands for "I will Somehow, in Someway, with Some effort Overcome All Rifts." Rifts representing the hurt, anger, pain, deceit, mistrust, the anguish and many more countless emotions we feel and experience, expressing as we have traveled through life. Understanding how to use these emotions as a compass and indicators to where we are in the moment of life so we can get back and work on to what serves us a peaceful state of mind. This helps us to understand we are responsible for our own healing and peace, no one else.

It is recognizing those things we hide and opt out of confronting may very well lead to our very own healing. At best in whatever scenario you are soaring, you are sharing with yourself the gentle sentiment to be kind and loving to yourself.

I Choose to SSSOAR

S.S.S.O.A.R is a movement honoring through thought, with what resonates with your spirit, and to what cleans you physically as you exist going about your day. It is in you learning new things regarding yourself and others, how you show up in your own affairs, how you treat yourself, and what you live for.

S.S.S.O.A.R is the movement of you and within you on display in your environment, mirroring you. If you are not soaring, why not? Why are you not becoming the very being you yearn to be? How do you celebrate you in unknown times? In celebrations and disappointments? Are you learning in all facets of your life? S.S.S.O.A.R is the process of becoming you my dove daily.

A dove historically has had many meanings. Among some Christian faiths the dove signifies the Holy Spirit. It was once a symbol of love in Greek mythology or a sign of purity in some parts of the world throughout the centuries. Some literature even shared doves are a sign for you to regain or become centered once again where you feel unbalanced, out of sync.

In this context, I have chosen the dove as a term of endearment. I find is interchangeable with love. The love you exude and represent. Are you being the very dove God, "It," or as I refer to as "Pa," has designed you to be?

Realize, you can't be any other way. As my doves, you soar in your own higher heights amongst your own flight pattern so you may be. You are a dove designed for a specific reason and you must exist in the very reason. Many are waiting for you to be the very unique, well equipped, intricately designed dove, creating with your wings, your journey, your special flight pattern. This is why I've coined you as such.

As for me, I serve as a medium, offering some insight or helpful hints directing you to a healthier you. Encouraging you to get to a better place and space in you and for you. I am a call to action for the betterment, the constant reminders in-thought as well as throughout your day. I am a sign of confirmation for you to go be for your audience. Those in need of you, waiting for you. I am an understanding the start begins with you. I am here to agitate your awakening. As I S.S.S.O.A.R in my own affairs, I share not offering solutions but suggestions, questions, analogies, metaphors to jog what you may already be questioning.

I want to inspire your already seen greatness. I am here to ignite you to S.S.S.O.A.R! My role is to continue to honor you, so you may honor others engaging you. Formulating whatever process you find yourself, you know how to manage you. I am a memo to you to always seek better in of support you.

Please understand, what best supports me won't look like yours, so create away as I share through poetry words to reflect on! Be the very resource to your very own cause. You are resourceful. I am a medium for encouragement when you cannot find the words of your own to encourage you; until you discover your own vernacular encouraging such a prize as you.

S.S.S.O.A.R, The Movement is to inspire you just enough to go find what you need, what is necessary to fulfill you. An initiative to go make you happen. Go build and create what supports you well. Practice until it reaches perfection of The best kept secret, You. Be your best advocate for you. This is why I share, why I have taken in thought and placed on paper. An awakening to your own cheering squad.

This type of love my dove, I would call is a daily, life long, never ending journey which will seem like work at first but will forever be intergraded and in your favor with your willingness to practice. It is getting down to knowing you so well, you shift with just a thought; you see, knowing how and where to move; you understand, with no turmoil. It is how you process you as you live.

I am here to help you get excited about the work you will have to do. Offering continuous encouragement and inspiration as you move through your work, mustering the energy to complete the work. It is a discovery process like no other! Where you, yes YOU, will have to find what supports you well. YOU will be challenged. YOU will get faint of heart. YOU will stop. YOU will get disappointed. You will have anger. The OUTCOME will not always meet your expectation. YOU will however, overcome having the commitment to know and learn you throughout it all. Keep you alive, full of love and peace with the mere steps YOU must take and create, sustaining YOU.

Acknowledgements

To all those who have come before me, I humbly bow and say, "Thank you." Forging your way gave me the permission to do the same. In the words of Maya Angelou I truly believe, "I come as one, coming as 10,000." I take you all with me on this journey. To my SSSOAR engineers, thank you, thank you, thank you for believing in something, in me that was yet unseen. You took a chance on me and for that I am grateful. See how far we have come!

To my Grace, what on earth can I say, I saw it through and it has been such an amazing journey. When I decided to acknowledge my gifts it has made room for me. Even though it feels just like the beginning, the purpose was always with me.

The struggle to commit was very real until I asked to teach me how to use something in my eyes as a great burden. My burden has been my grace. As you have led me, I have had the ability to lead my SSSOAR Village. I have cracked the door just enough to allow your Presence to come in.

To my SSSOAR core, John A. Jones, Lisa Rosemond, Malane Shani, Nes Brewer, I have shown up, hearing my call. I willingly agree to move in my very existence. I asked for all of you. You have been the echoes to a once agreed upon mission. From the bottom of a loving heart I share. Thank you.

Oh, to my family! Such a family as mine! You were built for me and I for you. There are not enough thank yous from the depth of my soul. To the head of our household, Earnest Womack Sr., I salute you. You are a loving husband, a dependable brother, a father to a community, and a loving daddy to me. I admire your stature, for you are my hero. Your ways carry on. I am a product of a strong father who engages me. Love you, Dad.

To my mother, Gwen Womack, who is the heart of our family. Your commit to love continues to inspire me. My first woman role model, you continue to amaze me. A mother to many, your care goes beyond the home you provided to my brother and I. Love you, Mom. You two together created some amazing children. Just know as Atlanta gets to know my brother and I, they know of you.

I Choose to SSSOAR

To my brother who is my best friend, two peas in a pod even though we are five years apart, I love you. You will always be my older, little brother. My protector and confidant, you have been my constant. Always having the best words to say. I am inspired by you and so proud of you. It has been a long time coming, but I am welcoming it.

To Tanea Womack, thank you for caring for my brother's heart. My brother is simply moved by you adding to the great women in our family. I admire you so. Continue to be the bright star you are. Love you.

To my little brother, Ryan Womack, I see you and super-duper proud to be your big sister. To my cousin Ashley, a sister I will call you! Girl it's been a soul searching story. We will have great stories to tell.

To my grandmothers, grandfathers, aunts, uncles, and cousins, I love you. You know who you are. I am proud of each and every one of you. Know I am never too far. Team Womack and Raleigh I will forever be. Aunt Jean, be ready. I will need your voice on stage. Just know your voice has always mattered to me. Upon your voice you carried me.

To Brother JL King; a well-orchestrated surprise, another like-minded being helping me to carry this vision through. The day I met you, discouragement was on the horizon. Thank you for your reception hearing the words I shared with you. It is just the beginning.

Dedication

I dedicate this book to those who recognize they are lost and would like to be found. They have come to their own understanding something must be done drastically different, giving themselves permission to pursue their own happiness.

They recognize something is just not quite right and is encouraged, through love or fear, to find their way back to self again. The seekers have come to a crossroad, understanding they must start from within. As Malane Shani always shared with me:

"Everything begins and ends with you."

CHAPTER ONE
And the Search
Begins...

Welcome to all things inspired with
Denell Porché

I am Denell

You are a visionary but first you must clean. I propose a question. How can you set a vision when you have no true clarity?

"As we heal, so will the world follow."

Sharing in this moment
All to encourage you on your flight . . .

Please, deep breathe with me
May I propose this to you?
How do you respond as chaotic moments come?

~ KNOW THIS ~

Ugly moments, what I like to call rifts, are opportune
times to
heal all unhealed wounds carried.
Why keep reliving?
You are your own self-healer.
Be willing. Become familiar with stillness.
Finding your own friendship with self in it.

Welcome Back

For you my dove exist in vulnerability again.

To my doves at flight,
May you find in those challenging times a space to reflect.
Realizing those things you must self-fix.
You are at your very beginning, now experiencing your present state of

Awareness

It's your own awakening.

CONGRATULATIONS!

Your search has always been. The difference?

You are in want

Now desiring to really know one self. Knowing something must shift, so why not go within?

I Choose to SSSOAR

What if trouble was only a figment

of your imagination?

Then one could conclude

Giving rise to what just might be true

The capability to define the contours of trouble

Possibly, changing the outlook of trouble

Confronting trouble

Telling where it can go that trouble

Minimizing those affairs trouble

Has defined for you

But that would be of course

If trouble was only a figment of your imagination

For it seems as trouble

Has convinced you

Of a reality you have succumbed to

You have turned a blind eye to what is real
Losing sight
Trouble be still
But of course
To check trouble at the door
You must have already known
Trouble was only a figment of your imagination

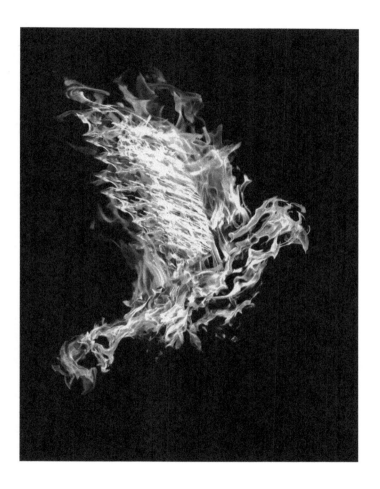

Practitioner you are
To what? Do you know?
Since practice makes perfect
You have nailed it with precision
Working those aspects
You really never thought existed
Practitioner of anything
For you have fallen for everything
Not taking the time to consider
Those things not made for the best me
It has become most common
To be a Practitioner with no thought
Rationalizing your self-worth
So others may shine
Dimming
What light you have for offer
So you may carry on
Practitioner you are
You do it so well
Some food for thought, though
And it's only a thought ...

I Choose to SSSOAR

When will you be a Practitioner?
In the routine
To supporting
Your better self,
How quick do we forget?
We create in any given mindset
Formulating our own environment
Designating third parties to who's to blame
Designing those things
We say we never made an agreement with
When in actuality we have put our signature stamp of
approval on it

We say it makes no sense
It can't be me in all of this
As it comes
For heavy is the burden
Just maybe we are the common denominator
To what life brings to us
But a fraction of second we spend on this one thought
How quick do we forget
We create in any given mind set
The who in you I find is an extension on how you do
Failing to understanding they work as two
One without the other
Gives rise to another
We may not fully understand
Doing our best to explain the imposter,
Confusing our audience
A minor glitch, we call life living
If willing to nurture them
Watching a greater improvement
We show up better knowing more of our self
Teaching others how to treat our self

I Choose to SSSOAR

Honoring the tools to build one self
Instructed as shown from within
to simply
How to fall in love with one's self

I Choose to SSSOAR

Layered by protection, vulnerability not an option
Keeping you hidden
Never going the distance
Not at your fullest for the layers help you sleep
Bringing false comfort
Slightly bothered, for you know
This is not how you want to be
If layers removed sharing the true side of you
The hurt supersedes
Keeping protection as unwanted friend for you
The cycle continues,
Alienating You
What to do?
But it's up to you
Layered by protection
It had served its time or two
Keeping to its word
Only now it hinders you
It cannot be in your everything
There is an attack
Due to all the layers of protection you perceive it as

It will take the Courage
Removing what layers helping you for a moment
So the option to vulnerability
May stretch its wings, attempting for you to
soar at best in your present existence

I Choose to SSSOAR

In the events of life, even the quiet makes much
Sound.
Wanting to offer resolution in most things.
Speaking with no fee, conjuring up the freedom for
Us to Be
Thoughtful is the Silence, showing much support
Through the Chaos
Guiding the path to Truth
So we may show up knowing just what to do
But as the show and dance go
We simply pass-by
Wanting to never take the time and chat for a while
Keeping us compromised
To those things we ask
Pleading with stretched out hands
If only when
Quiet serves as a forever best friend

I Choose to SSSOAR

Who do you belong to?
Have you ever asked this question?
Furthermore, to whom do you represent?
Reflect, Revisit, Revitalize
Your thoughts, your actions, your person
Again, who do you belong to?
How is it going for your person?
The thing you represent?
What part do you play?
Or are you even present today?
Replay, Reposition, Rethink
Your dialogue, your passion, your essence of you
I plea as I stand, to whom do you belong to?
At the end of the day, your answer will say?
Days end is moving swiftly
How do you represent?

Excuse me my Grace
I want to be like her
I need to know now, why I am not like her
Where do I fit, I am disgusted right now
Please forgive me my Grace
For not loving myself as of now
The images I see, why doesn't she look like me?
It seems to me she is who I should aim to be
The exterior I only see
It's praised for me to be
If I deviate from the mold
I'll most likely be out in the cold
I want to be honest with myself
Wanting only to see me
and nothing else

I Choose to SSSOAR

Confused about most things
I am losing the battle in how to love all myself
What on earth should I do?
Many times I sing the blues
I guess I will continue in the struggle
In my want to be of another
Excuse me my Grace
I want to be like her
I need to know now, why I am not like her
Where do I fit, I am disgusted right now
Please forgive me my Grace
For not loving myself as of now.

To heal all things chaotic in your life, you must heal you from within.

You are accountable for this most overlooked fact. Life doesn't just happen to you, but with you. You create the life that is currently presented to you. The important thing is you have the power of choice, the power to create different in your life.

But it must – it has to start from within.
And so it is ...

"To master yourself, you master the world."

Somehow – "I dream of being..." Please fill in the blank.

Most times I envision how I want to be in my life. I am observing my dream/ vision does not mirror what I am actually experiencing in life. Why?

Someway – "My goal is to make my dream a reality by..." Please fill in the blank.
I understand in order to achieve my dream/vision, I must create steps. I also must provide and seek resources to support me as I work my steps.

Some Effort – As I create (the work) my dream/vision, I will need an action statement to encourage me as I do my work. My action statement will support the thoughts I am thinking and what is being produced as I work my steps created above, reaching my dream/vision. Action statements begin with "I

I Choose to SSSOAR

am...", "I will...", "It is happening..." I am reminded to be kind to myself as I achieve my dream/vision. (Please refer to example action statements in the SSSOAR Wisdom of thought)

CHAPTER TWO

The Funny Things About Truth...

Sharing in this moment
All to encourage you on your flight

Walk with me

May I share this with you?
If truth really speaks to you, are you willing to listen,
receptive to its message?

~ Be Mindful ~

I Choose to SSSOAR

Mighty is the roar willing to be submissive to its own
Truth.
Recognizing the strength exuding from it,
even though ego may be hurt by its knowledge of
Truth.
Reception will be key for growth is the repercussion
if you take
a stance and dance with it.
Truth holds the greatest secret.
Most times sharing in subtle ways for we are
constantly in
pursuit of the cat and mouse game with
Truth.
To my doves at flight may you find reverence for
your own
Truth.
Embracing it in all its glory
Making room to converse with it every morning
Truth
Keeps you in a present state of awareness
Never letting you forget your greatness continues to
live with you
Rooting for you, knowing of the future successes
continuously seeking you

With what intent you seek
Nevertheless, it will bear fruit from the plants that
you seed
Carrying out your own agenda
Speaking volumes to what you think is hidden
Your reward for your own reaping
Whether you claim it or not
You are accountable for it, it proved its plot
Cost effective, no thought off
You sit with "Where did I go wrong?"
You continue to fail to see it is a continuation of your
own thoughts
Telling of your true intention so why are you mad?
You gave it life from the very beginning

Dream so your flight may follow
Turbulence along the way
Dream anyway
The glimpse to the possible
Given all to encourage what you perceive is
unthinkable
Manifest, is your intention
The truth of the matter
You hold to what will unfold
Truth rings
Be willing to bear to listen

I Choose to SSSOAR

I Choose to SSSOAR

Always in the making
Each day brings a new beginning
Muster all your stamina
For fear will do its best in its clever way of enticement
Move to your center
Grounded, for it knows of your better
Made in an image to whom is Greater.

Keep moving
For I will continue to say
Each day brings a new beginning
Challenging you, are you willing
To conduct your manner slightly different

So you may conform to a better you
All to understand
Each day brings a new beginning
An opportune time
To view yourself completely different

Truth is in the business of unveiling
what is unspoken
Prompting an opening to what is thought hidden
Seeking its own way finding better intentions
So those dangling from handed down tales
May discover their own truth amongst the chaos
It's funny how half told lies are served as principles
Thinking of only serving one owns purpose
Faults amongst the surface
Don't get to far ahead of yourself
You can only avoid it for a moment
Truth has the pleasure of showing what is thought
unseen
Fools, you think of those
You steady sing your lullabies too

I Choose to SSSOAR

The joke will eventually involve your tale in the end
Serving only what you believe
you should get kudos in
What then
Just know
Truth business may come with
unwanted investments
Unveiling what is unspoken
You won't be disappointed

The bells toll
Something is dying to be told
The fear keeps you from hearing
Even your exterior calls for special attention,
growing weary
I feel you slipping
Drowning in the abyss you call living
Avoiding what is to be had
Settling for the crumbs those have had
Why won't you confront it all?
So you may find your way back to the beginning
of it all
I see you are never here
Only a shell of person represents you my dear
Why may I ask your efforts are to convince me?
Even though the bells toll

I Choose to SSSOAR

It haunts you so
You are dying inside
And I truly miss you so

Listen, even when your heart has hardened.
Receive even if you don't agree
Hear even if you are quickly angered
See even when the veil is over your judgmental eyes
View even if you refuse to understand
Watch even if you are adamant in not taking a stance
Discuss even when the time may be challenging
Talk even if all refuse to acknowledge you
Speak, I plea when unspoken truth is not present

I Choose to SSSOAR

Fuck you truth
An enemy I am to you
You were never a friend
Who am I really to you?
I try and I try
I am in no need of you
I rather do my own thing
Finding my own way
A constant pain you are
Plaguing my life on a host of things
I would like to get by on how I do this life thing
No need of your intuition
You stick your nose in where it's not wanted
I am doing fine on my own
Can't you see, now move on
Truth you can't move me
I am sold on this very position
A conman you are to me
Having me to believe you are best for me
Truth be about your way
I have no time for you
Good day

I Choose to SSSOAR

You hurt me, even though you're always
concerned for *me*
You incite me, even though I do my best to hide from
the *presence of thee*
You bless me, although there are at times another
side of *you, you see*
You tease me, in a few times you have
made fun of *me*
You bestow on me, all those things I may have looked
over *casually*
You see me, even when I can no longer feel you
beneath *me*
You encourage me, even though at times I never ask
for *you*
You forgive me, when I wouldn't even accept
you
You create in me, when at last, I've learned to
embrace *you*

To know thy own truth is the beginning all things new. This is where understanding about you comes from. Becoming familiar with you so you may be the best storyteller of yourself. Why on earth would you allow others to tell of you? You become aware of the how in you so you may know the who of you.

Standing strong when truth comes, for it knows you. It wants to share with you. It will be up to you and your reception. It has to commune with you. The funny thing is, it will eventually catch up with you.

And so it is...

"Acknowledge what is true."

Somehow – "An attribute I refuse to see about myself is (are)…" Please Fill in the blank.

"I acquired this(these) attribute because…" Please feel in the blank.

Someway – "I have used this(these) attribute to my advantage by…" Fill in the blank.

"This attribute(s) has been a disadvantage by…" Fill in the blank.

I would like to make changes to this (these) attributes by…" Fill in the Blank.

I am creating the steps to work on adjusting the listed attribute(s) so when opportunity presents itself to create change, I will know how to use my steps.

Some Effort – As I create (the work) to change listed attributes, I will need an action statement to encourage me as I do my work. My action statement will support the thoughts I am thinking and what is being produced as I work my steps created above, causing change in my attributes.

Action statements begin with "I am…", "I will…", "It is happening…" I am reminded to be kind to myself as I achieve my change in attributes. (Please refer to example action statements in the SSSOAR Wisdom of thought)

_____

_____

_____

_____

_____

_____

_____

_____

_____

_____

_____

I Choose to SSSOAR

CHAPTER THREE

Oh to the Company

We Keep,

the Tribute...

Sharing in this moment
All to encourage you on your flight

Come commune with me

May I suggest some things?
How well do those who you call friends represent
you?

~Take Note~

If you can't self-examine, coming to some specific
conclusions; your peers, those who you claim as
friends are your best assets yet!

If you can stomach it, realizing your involvement
with them,
you will then be able to begin your adjustments even
if you will have to go at it without them.

In time you realize it's your surrounding cast who
may determine how well you will fare in all your
endeavors,
safe and very well in it.

I Choose to SSSOAR

To my doves at flight know the company you keep
comes in many hues,
bringing so many scenarios adding to or subtracting
to one's own well-being.
How is it that your company celebrates you?
What is it keeping them close to you?
How is it do they serve you?
Are they keeping you in a state of the blues?
Oh to the company we keep!
Influence becomes you.

I have had journeys with numerous people.
Only several know me well.
Y'all, it has been an upward climb.
So many couldn't tell.
From childhood, only one had made it.
From undergrad a couple grew.
As I have discovered, you can't travel with everyone.
Some of your numerous have snippets to play.
Remember, there might be a lesson.
For each and every one to take heed of, a blessing.
Once the communion has taken place.
Be steadfast and go your separate ways.
The best of the journey.
Continuous prayers for your traveling buddies.

My view on family...
They may be the downfall of you
Keeping you burdened
For what they won't show up in their own life to do
Expecting your involvement
Fixing where they have caused commotion
Where does it stop for you?

My view on family...
They may have all the success for you
Believing in those dreams you have
Making every effort to see you glad
Off in the race, providing the steps,
adding to your fate
What do you do?

No comparison, but may I ask two questions?

Which one represents you?
How does each one serve you?

If I reveal to you my hidden agenda
Please reveal to me your personal gain
If I reveal to you my inner most thoughts
Please consider to do the same
When I reveal my love for you
Be sure to embrace it in full
When I reveal my time with you
Come prepared to invest the same
As I reveal to you that I believe in you
You must know I am in you corner
As I reveal to you my inner most thoughts
Know I will give you the floor all the
same
Revelation builds our relationship
Moving us onward during our life phases
A synergy never changing

I Choose to SSSOAR

May I find a home in you?
When my world is in utter chaos
May you speak with heartfelt pleasantries?
When I have no one to call but you
May I receive peace of mind?
When in the world I can't understand it all
May I exist in needed rest?
When I feel like I can't go on
You see my friend you mean the world to me
Helping me to conquer many things perplexing me
I share with you
To remind you
Just how much I am in need of you

What in the world is your definition of
friendship?
Clearly we have miscommunicated our definition.
A sister I would love to call you,
A stranger is my thoughts of you.
To whom do I blame?
All aspects of you,
I assume, however, I mirror you.
So this is my conclusion about you,
We are a mess boo!
The havoc of our lives is always started by you,
But I must keep in mind I continue to entertain you.
I have no clue what is it about you,
Keeping me invested with you.
Most times you are a drug to me,
Fueling those things, always getting
the best of me.
Wanting to get away from you,
Turning right back around to engage you.
On a merry go round,
How do I get rid of you?

I Choose to SSSOAR

Opportunist they are to me
Taking their time, they know they will get something
from me
Never truly wanting to get to know me
I spread my legs for its time; I'm only good for one
thing
Convinced of this concept
I give of myself
Never second guessing
I play small getting a few moments of their
attention
I cry inside for I want more
But I keep it all inside
They might just run from me.
They really fail to notice that
I am a queen who was prayed for broken.
Maybe one day soon
They will come with heart
Wanting to know me
The "thing" we call God
Please be with me

Many times to those who we call friends you will have to learn to love them from a distance. Saying your farewells so you may continue on your own mission. Love never lost, but so many memories gained.

At the end of the day, most evolutions must shed to what served us at best, honoring those going through their own growing process. If it is time for someone to exit, send them their well wishes. Just know as you grow, it comes with a next set of companions.

And so it is ...

I Choose to SSSOAR

"To my company, I see you in me."

Somehow – "What are the qualities (positive and negative) I seek in relationships with friends, family, and significant others?" List. Why?

Someway – "The benefits I receive from each relationship listed are…" Fill in the blank.
"I will recognize the benefits of any relationship by…" Fill in the blank.
"I will handle unhealthy relationships by…" Fill in the blank.

Some Effort – As I create (the work) to maintain healthy relationships, I will need an action statement to encourage me as I do my work. My action statement will support the thoughts I am thinking and what is being produced as I work my steps created above, causing better relations with my friends, family and significant other.

Action statements begin with "I am...", "I will...", "It is happening..." I am reminded to be kind to myself as I achieve in how to create better relationship(s) with others. (Please refer to example action statements in the SSSOAR Wisdom of thought)

_____

_____

_____

_____

_____

_____

_____

_____

_____

_____

_____

_____

_____

_____

CHAPTER FOUR

The Art of Being,

A Salute to Your Very Own Being...

Sharing in this moment
All to encourage you on your flight
Come prevail with me
Impart on me, I am here and listening.
What do you look like really? Who do you claim to be
presently?

May I get to know you?

~Remember This~

"Be the best, the only, well acquainted Storyteller of your life. You are the epic of your journey. You are the vitality of your dreams. Convince me of your very existence who has conspired for you to be here in this very moment. Honoring the very best of you when you decide to show it. All of you matter, for you carry much weight. Being is the art of you, giving permission to see every potential of your being. "

To my doves at flight, S.S.S.O.A.R. yawl! Finding your somehow, in your someway, with your own effort to overcome all rifts preventing you from being your own greatness in your life. Rifts come in all forms, you forgetting most times, exposed to make you strong. Rifts are continuous, but your response to them doesn't have to be. Know it's only one of you so only you can be the very essence of you. Smile, for you are well on your way. Know I am proud of you.

I Choose to SSSOAR

Either way, I walk hand in hand
Co-creating with My Creator, ain't it grand?
Dreams, my Vision
My daily walk, my wrestling session.
At a glance, its seen, co-signing I'm closer than I
think.
My strokes have evolved, only leaving my
afterthought.
I am the progression, my world my inner stance.
As I see fit, it may change at any moment
The author of my own existence, I only entertain who
I am to be, spoken from a call only heard by me
Maintenance is key
The only goal is to be seen as me

May you realize it is your attempts that are worth all
the while.
Exposing you to unknown territory
Evolving you to the next phase of your journey
Finding your cause to each orchestrated effect.
Be willing to find your steps
All to catapult you to your very own greatness
The answers to your own dreams
Follows you
When you believe

I Choose to SSSOAR

May you know it is alright.
You are becoming
better for your own peace of mind.
Unveiled in due time,
If open, your greatest moment to respond much
differently.
Closer to what peace you seek,
Don't you see?
This is the art to be
Finding your true syncopation of things.
I see you laugh, it's comforting
Most don't know.
You're close, don't give up now
The sign is there.
Peace overcomes you,
Just know, I am so inspired by you.

May you find all things pleasant even when you feel
you're
soaring by your lonesome.
Your audience is captivated, your cheering squad,
your
inner whisper
Most times you may have to go at it alone
Causing a bit of fear seeking where to move on
Just know
Love surrounds you, imploring you
you can go on
It won't last long
This part is necessary
So you may learn a pressing lesson

I Choose to SSSOAR

Creativity exudes you for you have committed to the
process of finding the truest you
Understanding it's a constant discovery
Only to maintain inner beauty
Those who whisper, is only a side note
Grappling with their own understanding
Mesmerized by your radiant energy
In time they will receive what you are
emitting
Always in a consistent pursuit of self
Opening the door to meeting an exceptional self
Welcome to the roused you
Be the light
You are a vision to be
Your light, lighting others
Certifying how we oughta be

I Choose to SSSOAR

You are legendary so why on earth exist as ordinary
The extra becomes you
Telling of great assets bestowed upon you
It will take you to show up as you
The love will carry on when you have transitioned on
Leaving behind of those great things
You backed people to be themselves and dance on
You are legendary
Never playing small
You have come to be the very thing it's told to not
speak on
Bright as a star
It took you
Bringing all things full circle
Adding the necessary step so many may continue on
You are legendary so why on earth exist as ordinary

So many faces all belonging to the same breath.
A collage representing the diversity of your inner
spirit.
Isn't it amazing the many faces you wear?
Many times providing the platform to share an
intended message,
so you may mingle amongst the masses, sharing
perspective.
This is one of many things making you so great.
You are the exact replica of an intentional objective.
Establishing the framework for you to continually
compose in.
Compose away my doves, you are endless.
For you still remain the very love, bestowed

I Choose to SSSOAR

When it gets down to it
One day you must decide
Contributing to society with constructive purpose
The next step
Formulating ways to meet your greatest potential
Determining what your greatness will be

I want to know of you. So I may begin to speak of the greatness exhibited by you. Pour into me so I may carry you with me, beyond those times when I can't find the best in me. Your aura I feel, for you have managed to be all you can be. Your love I stand in, for you have given yourself permission to see the vulnerable side of things. A burden no more, you have learned how to live, representing you in everything.

And so it is...

"Tell your own story"

Somehow – "I am…" Fill in the blank.

Someway – "I will share my own story of who I am by…" Fill in the blank.

I have every opportunity to learn who I am with life. In every situation, I have something new to learn about me.

Some Effort – As I commit (the work) to learning myself, I will need an action statement to encourage me as I do my work. My action statement will support the thoughts I am thinking and what is being produced as I work my steps created above, learning about me.

Action statements begin with "I am…", "I will…", "It is happening…" I am reminded to be kind to myself as I am exposed to situations where something is

learned new about me. (Please refer to example
action statements in the SSSOAR Wisdom of thought)

_____

_____

_____

_____

_____

_____

_____

_____

_____

_____

_____

_____

_____

_____

_____

I Choose to SSSOAR

"Consideration welcomes opportunity."

IN CONCLUSION

Reflection

My Way to You

I want you to know the most precious thing on this earth is you. Always be in your own art of self-discovery so the present you may show up as you in all you do.

You deserve your own best. You deserve the opportunity to teach others in how to show up for you. You deserve the life you have always wanted. You deserve to say no to those things not complimenting your inner being, your spirit resonance. You deserve the power of choice. You deserve those things you have told yourself you can't achieve. You deserve. You are worthy.

You are the very example of I can. You, the potentiate of your own evolution. It's for you. You so deserve.

I Choose to SSSOAR

I want you to know the very existence of me is contingent on you. I am deserving of you for you tell of the greatest story of us. You deserve the peace your soul searches to exist in. You deserve the utmost respect defined by you. You deserve the healing to those things causing or have caused the most pain. You deserve the present state of mind so you truly can intimately fall in love with the day. You deserve a community mirroring the idea of you. You deserve all of what has not been presented to you as of yet. You deserve no form of hindrance. You deserve. You are worthy. You are the very example of I am. You, the potentiate of your own evolution. It's for you. You so deserve.

I want you to know the day you decide you deserve, you have found the very love you have been seeking, giving yourself the very permission and accountability to your own success. To all my doves flying higher heights, sssoar. You so deserve. I so deserve. This is what I have found in my own self- discovery. So I share with you. I approve, you are permitted to grasp this concept wholeheartedly.

"Know, most precious on this earth,
you."

~ You've been Smooched,

Denell Porché

I Choose to SSSOAR

"Let the mediation of my heart be acceptable to thy soul. Let the words of my mouth be receptive to those who all hear. Let the actions of my person be acceptable towards thy own healing. Let the thoughts I care to speak add to the catalyst to each ones change."

~ Smooches from my heart to yours,

Denell Porché

About the Author

A conglomerate of many gifts, Denell Porché was born and raised in Cincinnati, Ohio. A graduate of the prestigious Tuskegee University, Denell pursued a Bachelor of Science degree in Animal and Poultry Science where she continued some graduate work in veterinary science. With the joy of music in her heart, she decided to move to Atlanta, Georgia in 2006, pursuing a Master in Education in Secondary Science in Biology with the hidden agenda to grace the performance stage.

While teaching in the Cobb County school system, in her leisure time, she began her investment in the Arts. It started with her love for mime. She was able to mime through Speechless Mime ministry at Elizabeth Baptist Church.

Even though her school of music began as a child, it was nurtured while an undergraduate at Tuskegee with the *Golden Voices*, and honed with Pitch Perfect

I Choose to SSSOAR

Studios under the direction of John A. Jones and Lisa Rosemond at Jane Smith's Studio.

Acknowledging her gift in voice and writing, she began involving herself in what Atlanta had to offer. Enjoying opportunities like singing background vocals, participating in musicals, contributing to artist tracks, writing poetry in her spare time, and opening for a local Atlanta artist in 2014.

Denell also was a co-host for a radio show called *The Earnest Womack Live Show*, which blossomed into her own platform, offering *Afternoon Inspirations* on the New Sensation Station Network in Atlanta, Georgia. In this moment, Denell decided it was time to grace the stage sharing her own artistry. While developing her own voice on paper and through sound, she decided to obtain her Associate Degree in Nursing, funding her purpose as an artist.

Denell believes in the very idea of encouragement, rooted in her favorite scripture from the Bible, Proverbs 15:4. She believes encouragement comes in all forms and goes beyond the laws of religion.

Denell's passion is women's initiatives, inspired by the process of healing those things necessary for women to reach their greatest potential – "As we heal, so will the world follow."

Through song and poetry, Denell wants women to understand they are uniquely precious. Owning this very concept give each individual woman permission to heal through their most challenging times, soaring to their own highest height.

Wisdom of Thought
Action Statements

To my doves, listed below are states in action to show and say, supporting what exact growth you would like to make, to change/confirm what you see, and/or providing kindness to yourself while experiencing some type of realization about yourself. Use these at leisure or use these as examples to create your own.

"I am wrestling my dream to reality."

"I am willing to progress through all seasons, acknowledging love in many forms."

"I know, most precious on this earth is me."

"I will create and know peace amongst the chaos."

"This is happening in order to discover a better me."

"I will be kind and understanding to truth as it presents itself."

"I am supplied with every tool to create right now."

"I am willing to forgive myself when I see unintended outcomes."

"I am beautiful even in this moment."

"I will be presented with situations to challenge me for the better."

"I am showing up at my best."

"I am what I decide in my mind to be."

"It so happens I am hurting, but I recognize I am safe."

"I have made a mistake; I am a learner in this moment."

"I am understanding one quality about me today."

I Choose to SSSOAR

"I will provide one forgiving act each day to a person who I perceive as doing wrong to me."

"I am so beautiful today."

"I will define qualities supportive for me in friendships."

"In what I am creating is happening in what I think, how I speak, and to what I am feeling."

For more inspirational works and

booking information for Denell Porché,

visit www.denellporche.com